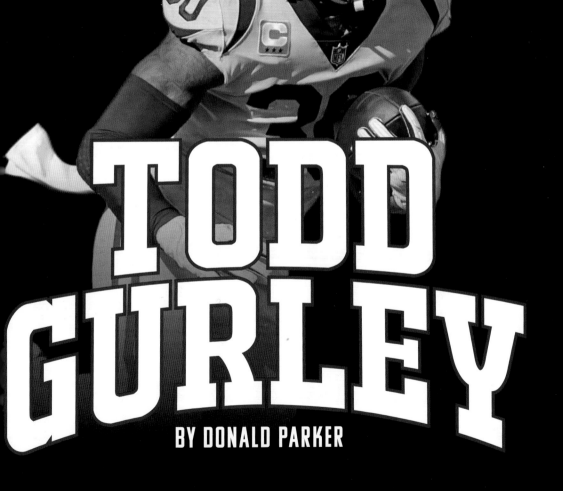

GRIDIRON GREATS
PRO FOOTBALL'S BEST PLAYERS

TODD GURLEY

BY DONALD PARKER

GRIDIRON GREATS
PRO FOOTBALL'S BEST PLAYERS

AARON DONALD

AARON RODGERS

ALVIN KAMARA

ANTONIO BROWN

DREW BREES

J.J. WATT

JULIO JONES

KHALIL MACK

ODELL BECKHAM JR.

ROB GRONKOWSKI

RUSSELL WILSON

TODD GURLEY

TOM BRADY

VON MILLER

GRIDIRON GREATS

PRO FOOTBALL'S BEST PLAYERS

TODD GURLEY

BY DONALD PARKER

MASON CREST

Mason Crest
450 Parkway Drive, Suite D
Broomall, Pennsylvania 19008
(866) MCP-BOOK (toll-free)
www.masoncrest.com

First printing
9 8 7 6 5 4 3 2 1

ISBN (hardback) 978-1-4222-4343-5
ISBN (ebook) 978-1-4222-7472-9

Cataloging-in-Publication Data on file with the Library of Congress

Developed and Produced by National Highlights Inc.
Editor: Andrew Luke
Interior and cover design: Jana Rade, impact studios
Production: Michelle Luke

NATIONAL
HIGHLIGHTS

CONTENTS

KEY ICONS TO LOOK FOR:

 Words to Understand: These words with their easy-to-understand definitions will increase the reader's understanding of the text while building vocabulary skills.

 Sidebars: This boxed material within the main text allows readers to build knowledge, gain insights, explore possibilities, and broaden their perspectives by weaving together additional information to provide realistic and holistic perspectives.

 Educational Videos: Readers can view videos by scanning our QR codes, providing them with additional educational content to supplement the text. Examples include news coverage, moments in history, speeches, iconic sports moments, and much more!

 Text-Dependent Questions: These questions send the reader back to the text for more careful attention to the evidence presented there.

 Research Projects: Readers are pointed toward areas of further inquiry connected to each chapter. Suggestions are provided for projects that encourage deeper research and analysis.

 Series Glossary of Key Terms: This back-of-the-book glossary contains terminology used throughout this series. Words found here increase the reader's ability to read and comprehend higher-level books and articles in this field.

WORDS TO UNDERSTAND

CALIBER – degree of capacity or competence; ability

CAMPAIGN – a systematic course of aggressive activities for some specific purpose

CREDENTIALS – anything that provides the basis for confidence, belief, credit, etc.

ELITE – the choice or best of anything considered collectively, as of a group or class of persons

CHAPTER 1

GREATEST MOMENTS

TODD GURLEY'S NFL CAREER

The Los Angeles Rams have waited a long time for a player like Todd Gurley to help take them to the next level as one of the league's *elite* teams. Not since Steven Jackson, who led the team in rushing eight years in a row (2005–2012), has a running back of this quality played for the Rams. Since being selected by the then St. Louis Rams with the 10th pick in the 2015 NFL Draft, Gurley has led the team in rushing in each of his four seasons through 2018.

Gurley has twice been recognized league-wide for his offensive play, once in his rookie season of 2015 and again as a veteran player in 2017. He has become an important part of the team's offensive plans, helping lead the Rams back to the top of the pack. Gurley has averaged more than 82 points a season or nearly fourteen touchdowns (rushing and receiving) in each of the four seasons he has played.

Peers and experts recognize Gurley as one of the elite running backs in the NFL (National Football League). His style and efficiency as a running back have drawn comparisons to Le'Veon Bell, Frank Gore, Larry Johnson, and Arian Foster. His forty-four career rushing touchdowns already place him in the top 100 among all running backs in the history of the NFL (ranked 96).

Gurley has been compared to former Pittsburgh Steeler running back Le'Veon Bell.

Gurley has far outclassed the other members of his 2015 draft class. These include runners like Melvin Gordon drafted five picks after him by the San Diego (now Los Angeles) Chargers, fellow SEC (Southeastern Conference) member T.J. Yeldon, chosen by the Jacksonville Jaguars, Ameer Abdullah from the University of Nebraska (drafted by the Detroit Lions), and David Johnson, drafted by the Arizona Cardinals. Johnson and Gurley are among only thirteen players in the history of the NFL to rush for more than 750 yards (685.8 m) and record 750 yards (685.8m) in receiving for a single season.

As Gurley goes as a skilled runner, so go the fortunes of the Los Angeles Rams. As long as he stays healthy, great success should come for both him and the team. A four-year contract extension that he signed in 2018, with an optional fifth year, worth a total of $87 million in salary and bonuses, should ensure that Gurley will be a member of the Los Angeles Rams for a long time to come. If he continues to play at the exceptional level that he is playing, he may possibly become a candidate for inclusion in football's Hall of Fame in Canton, OH.

GURLEY'S GREATEST CAREER MOMENTS

HERE IS A LIST OF SOME OF THE KEY MOMENTS IN THE STANDOUT CAREER OF TODD GURLEY DURING HIS TIME IN THE NFL SO FAR:

FIRST NFL 100-YARD (91.44 M) RUSHING GAME

Gurley, playing in his second NFL game against the Arizona Cardinals on October 4, 2015, established himself as a runner other teams need to take notice of and watch. He rushed for more than 100 yards (91.44 m) for the first time in his NFL career, a feat that he has accomplished seventeen times in his career to date. Gurley's totals in the 24–22 victory were 146 yards (133.5 m) gained on nineteen rushing attempts, an average of 7.7 yards (7.04 m) a carry. He also caught two passes for 15 yards (13.72 m).

Gurley gets his career off and running in a performance against the Arizona Cardinals, October 4, 2015, that led to his first 100-yard rushing game.

FIRST NFL 200-YARD (182.88 M) RUSHING GAME

Gurley accomplished something in his fourth season in the NFL that has only been accomplished by a select number of players in the history of the league. Gurley rushed for 208 yards (190.2 m) in an October 14, 2018, game against the Denver Broncos. His twenty-eight rushing attempts yielded him a yards-per-carry average of 7.4 (6.8 m per carry). He also scored two touchdowns. His efforts helped lead the Rams to a sixth consecutive win in the 2018 season, 23–20.

Gurley's efforts in 2018 were a big reason for the success of the Rams. He hung 208 yards (190.2 m) on the Broncos to earn a game ball from Rams coach Sean McVay.

FIRST NFL 1,000-YARD (914.4 M) RUSHING SEASON (2015)

Gurley proved the Rams right in selecting him as the first running back with the tenth pick of the 2015 NFL Draft. He proved himself ready to move from college ball to the challenges of the professional gridiron. Averaging 4.83 yards (4.4 m) per carry, he racked up 1,106 yards (1,011.3 m) on 229 rushing attempts. These totals were tops among all rookie running backs and positioned Gurley for future greatness at the position. His effort also helped open up the Ram's running game, adding a needed offensive weapon.

Gurley's rookie season in the NFL was his first 1,000-yard (914.4 m) rushing season, as seen in these highlights from 2015.

FIRST CAREER RUSHING TOUCHDOWN

Gurley rushed for 146 yards (133.5 m) in his first NFL 100-yard (91.2 m) performance in a game against the Arizona Cardinals, which the Rams won. He followed that performance with a 159-yard (145.4 m) effort against the Packers the following week. He had not, however, scored a touchdown (rushing or receiving). This changed when he was given the ball in the following game, the fourth of his career. The 24–6 victory over Cleveland on October 25, 2015, was fueled in part by his 19 carry, 128-yard (117.04 m) game, which included the first and second rushing touchdowns of his NFL career.

In an October 25, 2015, game against the Cleveland Browns, Gurley takes a handoff from QB (quarterback) Nick Foles near the goal line to take it in one yard for his first career touchdown. [Begin at the 2:47 min. mark in the video.]

FIRST CAREER RECEIVING TOUCHDOWN

Gurley had scored sixteen touchdowns rushing in the prior two seasons leading up to the beginning of the 2017 NFL season. He began the 2017 season with a rushing touchdown in a 46–9 opening game victory over the Indianapolis Colts. He had not, as of that point, caught a football for a touchdown. That changed in his second game, against Washington. He caught three passes in the eventual 27–20 loss, including one for 18 yards (16.5 m) and his first receiving touchdown. He finished the season with six receiving touchdowns.

Gurley scores his first receiving touchdown in a September 17, 2017, game versus Washington in dramatic fashion, leaping over a defender on his way to an 18-yard (16.5 m) score.

NFL RUSHING LEADER IN A SEASON

2017 was a great year for Gurley. He led all rushers with 1,305 yards (1,193.3 m) and had 2,093 all-purpose yards (1,913.8 m). He also found the end zone thirteen times, thus leading the league in touchdowns as well. Except for the 2016 season, Gurley has rushed for ten or more touchdowns in three of his first four seasons. He has moved into the top 100 for career rushing TDs (touchdowns) and is on a pace to become the all-time rushing TD leader.

Gurley has a talent for finding the end zone from the ground, as seen in this highlight of his effort against the San Francisco 49ers, September 21, 2017. He scored two of his thirteen rushing touchdowns for the 2017 season in this game (and added one more through the air).

NAMED NFL AP OFFENSIVE ROOKIE OF THE YEAR (2015)

Gurley's rookie **campaign** in the NFL was a successful one. He appeared in just thirteen of the sixteen Rams games but still established his **credentials** as a future star in the NFL. He posted 1,106 yards (1,011.3 m) rushing to lead all rookie running backs in 2015. He also led rookie RBs (running backs) in rushing attempts (229), rushing touchdowns (10), yards per carry (4.8 or 4.4 meters per carry), and yards per game (85.1 or 77.8 meters per game). He finished third in rushing among all NFL RBs and did more than enough to earn honors as the Associated Press Offensive Rookie of the Year.

His numbers in his first NFL season were outstanding, separating him from his fellow rookies and placing him on the road to future greatness.

the league in rushing and rushing TDs with 1,305 yards (1,193.3 m) and thirteen touchdowns. He also had 64 receptions for 788 yards (720.6 m) and six touchdowns. He led the league in all-purpose yards with 2,093 (1,913.8 m). His totals, along with the Rams' 11–5 finish and first playoff appearance since 2004, helped him finish the year as the Offensive Player of the Year.

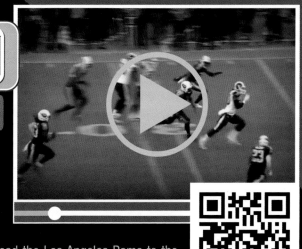

Gurley improved greatly in 2017 to lead the Los Angeles Rams to the playoffs for the first time in thirteen years, and as a result of his effort, win player of the year recognition for offense.

It is still a long way away, but enshrinement at the Football Hall of Fame is a distinct possibility if Gurley's career stays on its current trajectory.

TEXT-DEPENDENT QUESTIONS:

1. What year did Gurley win the NFL's Offensive Player of the Year award?
2. How many yards did he rush for in 2017? How many all-purpose (total) yards did he have for the 2017 season?
3. How many points has Gurley averaged each season since being drafted by the Rams in 2015? How many touchdowns has he averaged?

WORDS TO UNDERSTAND

COMBINE – an event at which scouts from the teams in a professional sports league gather to evaluate players in preparation for choosing which players to draft

COURT – to seek to attract (as by solicitous attention or offers of advantages)

DISSUADE – to advise (a person) against something

ECLIPSE – surpass

SIGNATURE – something (such as a tune, style, or logo) that serves to set apart or identify

CHAPTER 2

THE ROAD TO THE TOP

GURLEY ON THE GRIDIRON

Todd Jerome Gurley II was born on August 3, 1994, in Baltimore, MD. He was raised by his parents, Todd Jerome Gurley and Darlene Simmons, in Tarboro, North Carolina, a town of 11,229 residents (as of 2016), located on the state's coastal plains, twenty-five miles north of the city of Greenville. Gurley has four brothers, named Davon, Shannon, Princeton, and Tarik. During a game at the University of Georgia, he paid tribute to his father by having the Roman numerals "II" added to the back of his jersey. Gurley now wears the Roman numerals on his jersey for the Rams.

Gurley seemed destined for a career in professional football as he grew to be 6 feet 1 inch (1.85 m) tall and a weight of 205 pounds (93 kg) by the time he was being recruited in his senior year of high school. He grew up in Tarboro, away from the distractions and people that might dissuade him from sticking to his training and pursuing his dream.

Gurley has rushed, through the 2018 NFL season, for 4,547 yards (4,157.8 m) and forty-six touchdowns in four seasons as a member of the St. Louis and Los Angeles Rams. He also has 1,883 receiving yards (1,721.8 m) and ten receiving touchdowns. Gurley's forty-six rushing touchdowns rank him ninth among all active players in rushing TDs.

Gurley's **signature** move is borne of his leaping ability. Although it can be dangerous, he is prone to jumping over the top of tacklers to gain more yards or score touchdowns. This fearlessness is what makes him one of the most exciting players to watch. Jumping shows that he is willing to give everything to win a game, including putting his body at risk through the air if it means an extra yard.

HIGH SCHOOL

Gurley attended his hometown Tarboro High School (THS—Nickname: "Vikings") in Tarboro, NC, as a freshman in the fall of 2009. He became a regular starter on the team beginning in his junior year in 2010. Gurley rushed the ball for 1,472 yards (1,346 m) and twenty-six touchdowns. He was an important part of the school winning the North Carolina 2A State Football Championship that year. In Gurley's senior year at THS, he **eclipsed** his rushing total in his junior year, rushing the football for 2,600 yards (2,377.4 m) on the ground and thirty-eight touchdowns.

The Vikings repeated as Division 2A champions and for his efforts in 2011, Gurley was named AP Player of the Year for the State of North Carolina. He also ran track in addition to playing football in high school. Gurley competed in the sprints and hurdles and found a spot on the Team USA youth team for the 2011 World Youth Championships. He also placed second overall in the North Carolina High School Athletic Association's Division 2A track meet in 2011 in the 100-meter dash.

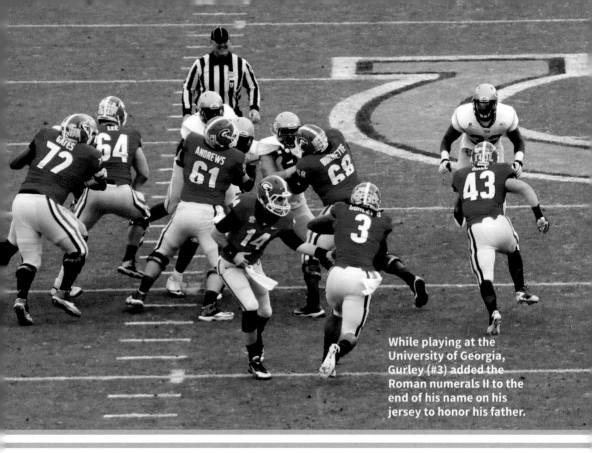

While playing at the University of Georgia, Gurley (#3) added the Roman numerals II to the end of his name on his jersey to honor his father.

In addition to being named player of the year in 2011, Gurley was named the All-Area Offensive Player of the Year in 2010 by the Rocky Mount Telegram newspaper. He played defensive back in addition to running back for THS, accumulating seventy-nine tackles, one interception, and a forced fumble. Gurley led the Vikings to consecutive state championships in his junior (2010) and senior years (2011), and a runner-up finish in his sophomore year (2009).

Gurley's speed on the track and rushing totals on the football field made him a four-star recruit. This rating was given to him by all the top high-school rating services, including Rivals, 247Sports, Scout, and ESPN. Nationally, Gurley was considered the fifth best running back in the country and was courted with recruiting offers from the following schools:

- Auburn University (Nickname: "Tigers"), Auburn, AL
- Clemson University (Nickname: "Tigers"), Clemson, SC
- Duke University (Nickname: "Blue Devils"), Durham, NC
- University of Georgia (Nickname: "Bulldogs"), Athens, GA
- North Carolina State University (Nickname: "Wolfpack"), Raleigh, NC

Gurley chose to attend the University of Georgia at Athens (Nickname: "Bulldogs") of the Southeastern Conference (SEC) and signed a letter of commitment on January 13, 2012.

In addition to football, Gurley also ran track in high school, competing in the sprints and hurdles.

COLLEGE

Gurley entered the University of Georgia in the fall of 2012, initially as a backup to the starting running back Ken Malcome. He saw playing time in a September 1, 2012, nonconference game against the University of Buffalo Bulls. Although Gurley did not start, he rushed the ball eight times for 100 yards (91.4 m) and two touchdowns. He also returned a kickoff 100 yards for a touchdown. Gurley's three scores helped the Bulldogs beat the Bulls by the score of 45–23.

By the second game of the 2012 season, Gurley became a starter and started in twelve of the season's fourteen games (causing Malcome to transfer to Southern Illinois University at the end of the season). Gurley finished the season with 222 rushes for 1,385 yards (1,266.4 m) as the number five ranked Bulldogs lost to the University of Alabama Crimson Tide in the SEC Championship. Georgia went on to defeat the University of Nebraska Cornhuskers (of the Big Ten Conference) in the Capital One Bowl. Gurley's season rushing total was the highest for a University of Georgia freshman since former Heisman award winner Hershel Walker rushed for 1,616 yards (1,477.7 m), thirty-two years prior in 1980.

Gurley was named to the All-SEC First Team and was joined by another SEC freshman, T.J. Yeldon from the University of Alabama (who was selected by Jacksonville in the 2015 draft with the thirty-sixth pick). Gurley went on to play ten games in his sophomore year, rushing for 989 yards (904.3 m) and ten touchdowns and catching thirty-seven passes for 441 yards (403.3 m) and six TDs.

A suspension imposed by the NCAA caused Gurley to miss part of his junior year season. Although he played in just six games in 2014, his yards per attempt were higher that season than the previous two (7.2). Gurley also had a higher yards-per-game average

TODD GURLEY DRAFT DAY

Todd Gurley was selected by St. Louis (now Los Angeles) with the tenth pick in the first round of the 2015 NFL Draft.

NFL DRAFT DAY 2015
SIGNIFICANT ACCOUNTS

- The 2015 NFL draft was held at the Auditorium Theater and Grant Park located in Chicago, IL. It was the first time the draft was not held in New York City since 1965.

- Gurley was the first running back drafted in the 2015 NFL Draft.

- Gurley and Melvin Gordon (from the University of Wisconsin), were the only running backs selected in the first round (Gordon was drafted by the San Diego, now Los Angeles, Chargers with the fifteenth pick).

- Gurley was one of eighteen running backs selected in the 2015 NFL Draft.

- For just the sixth time in NFL history, quarterbacks were selected with the first (Jameis Winston, Florida State) and second (Marcus Mariota, Oregon) overall picks. The 2013 Heisman Trophy winner Winston went to Tampa Bay, while 2014 Heisman winner Mariota went to Tennessee.

- Defensive Back (DB), which includes Cornerbacks (CB) and Safeties (S), was the most commonly selected position. Forty-six were selected in the 2015 Draft.

- The first defensive back selected was Trae Waynes, a CB from Michigan State University, who went in the first round with the eleventh pick to the Minnesota Vikings. Damarious Randall from Arizona State University was the first safety selected with the thirtieth selection by the Green Bay Packers.

- The Cleveland Browns had the most selections in the draft with twelve.

- The Carolina Panthers and San Diego Charges had the fewest selections in the draft with five each.

over the six games he played—151.8 versus 98.9—than in each of the previous two seasons. At the end of the 2014 season, he decided to give up his last year of eligibility and declared for the 2015 NFL draft.

Year	Tm	G	Rush	Yds	Rush TD	Y/A	Y/G	Rec	Yds	Y/R	Rec TD	Fmb
2012 (Fr.)	Georgia ("Bulldogs")	14	222	1,385	17	6.2	98.9	16	117	7.3	0	0
2013 (So.)	Georgia ("Bulldogs")	10	165	989	10	6.0	98.9	37	441	11.9	6	0
2014 (Jr.)	Georgia ("Bulldogs")	6	123	911	9	7.4	151.8	12	57	4.8	0	0
Career		30	510	3,285	36	6.4	109.5	65	615	9.5	6	0

Gurley became the starting RB for the Bulldogs in just his second career college game.

NCAA SUSPENSION

Gurley began his junior year in 2014 on a bad note. In October of that season the NCAA suspended him for four games for a rules violation. The violation involved his acceptance of nearly $3,000 for autographs and the sale of memorabilia over a two-year period. The NCAA does not permit student-athletes to earn money outside of the scholarships they receive to play football. It also does not permit student-athletes to profit from their status as college players. Gurley took his punishment in stride and returned ready to contribute to the team and raise his profile for NFL scouts.

Gurley served his punishment and returned to the gridiron for the Bulldogs to gain 911 yards (833.01 m) and score nine rushing touchdowns. This helped him become the first running back drafted in 2015.

NFL

2015 NFL COMBINE

Gurley participated in the 2015 NFL scouting combine on February 21, 2015, held at Lucas Oil Stadium in Indianapolis, IN (home to the Indianapolis Colts). He was one of twenty-nine running backs invited to participate in the workouts. An ankle injury that he had suffered in his sophomore season kept Gurley from fully participating in the combine. As a result, he participated in two drills: the 40-yard (36.6 m) dash, which he ran in 4.52 seconds, and the bench-press. Gurley pressed 225 pounds (102.06 kg) seventeen times.

Gurley was favorable compared to Marshawn Lynch, the 2007 first round pick (number twelve by the Buffalo Bills), according to NFL draft analyst Mike Mayock, a former player himself:

"I like the Marshawn Lynch comparison. St. Louis wants to win games the same way that Seattle and San Francisco do in the same division. That is by running the football and playing great defense and special teams. Gurley has Olympic-type speed. I love this pick for St. Louis, which already has a great defense, and Gurley will help out Nick Foles," said Mayock.

He was measured at 6 feet 1 inch (1.85 m), 222 pounds (100.7 kg), with an arm length of 31½ inches (0.8 m) and hands that measured 10 inches (0.3 m). His strengths include a blend of both speed and power. Scouts admired his ability to explode through his runs and an ability to keep moving even after initial contact. They were concerned that his ankle injury could be a problem for him later in his career. Overall, NFL scouts felt that Gurley would be able to overcome any weaknesses he might have and turn into a premier running back in the NFL.

At the 2015 NFL Combine, scouts were comparing Gurley to NFL star Marshawn Lynch.

Melvin Gordon of Wisconsin was the second RB taken in the 2015 NFL draft.

TOP ROOKIE RUNNING BACK COMPARISON

Gurley was chosen as the first running back in the 2015 NFL Draft, with the tenth pick overall. He was selected five picks ahead of Doak Walker award winner (an award given to college football's top running back) Melvin Gordon of the University of Wisconsin. Gurley was also selected ahead of fellow SEC running back T.J. Yeldon of the University of Alabama.

Gurley's rookie numbers stood out over the eighteen other running backs taken in the 2015 NFL Draft. He rushed for more yards, had more rushing touchdowns, the most rushing attempts, and the best yards per game average.

Player	Team	G	GS	Rush	Yds	Rush TD	Lng	Y/A	Y/G	Rec	Yds	Y/R	Rec TD	Lng
Todd Gurley	STL/LAR	13	12	229	1106	10	71	4.8	85.1	21	188	9.0	0	31
T.J. Yeldon	JAX	12	12	182	740	2	45	4.1	61.7	36	279	7.8	1	67
Melvin Gordon	SDG/LAC	14	13	184	641	0	27	3.5	45.8	33	192	5.8	0	18
Ameer Abdullah	DET	16	9	143	597	2	36	4.2	37.3	25	183	7.3	1	36
David Johnson	ARI	16	5	125	581	8	47	4.6	36.3	36	457	12.7	4	55

His numbers for his rookie season helped him become one of only five rookies to be named to the Pro Bowl for the 2015–2016 NFL season. He also beat out former Heisman trophy winner Jameis Winston, quarterback of the Tampa Bay Buccaneers, to win Rookie of the Year honors.

Gurley was suspended in his junior season at Georgia for accepting money from outside sources. The issue of NCAA athletes on scholarship receiving payment has spurred many lawsuits and has been argued in front of the United States Supreme Court.

EQUAL JUSTICE UNDER LAW

RESEARCH PROJECT:

There has always been an issue for college athletes when it comes to accepting money from sources other than scholarships. This issue was the focus of a lawsuit between several former athletes and the NCAA that was taken as far as the U.S. Supreme Court. Gurley's suspension for receiving payments has affected other players who were also similarly suspended but went on to get drafted in the NFL. Research to find several other recent draft picks (including a quarterback who won the Heisman trophy), and make a chart showing how many games they were suspended by the NCAA, the year they chose to enter the NFL draft, whether they finished college before or after leaving for the draft, and whether they are still active in the league.

TEXT-DEPENDENT QUESTIONS:

1. Where was Gurley born? Where did he grow up?
2. How many schools made recruiting offers to Gurley? Where did he choose to play college football?
3. How many games did the NCAA suspend him for in 2014? What was the reason for his suspension?

WORDS TO UNDERSTAND

ADVERSITY – a state or instance of serious or continued difficulty or misfortune

FORMULA – a method or procedure for doing or attaining something

SOPHOMORE SLUMP – a term used to describe the state of an athlete who is achieving poor results in a second season as compared to his or her first

SUBPAR – below an average, usual, or normal level, quality, or the like

CHAPTER 3

ON THE FIELD

GURLEY'S NFL ACCOMPLISHMENTS

Gurley has had quite an impact in his four years with the Rams. He has been honored frequently and has received the following honors and awards through the 2018–2019 NFL season:

- Named the 2015 AP Offensive Rookie of the Year
- Named the 2017 AP Offensive Player of the Year
- Three-time Pro Bowl selection (2015, 2017, 2018)
- Named All-Pro in three seasons:
    - 2015–Second Team (AP)
    - 2017–First Team (AP)
    - 2017–First Team (Pro Football Writers Association)
    - 2017–First Team (Pro Football Focus)
    - 2017–First Team (Sporting News)
    - 2018–First Team (AP)

GRIDIRON GREATS

TODD GURLEY
LOS ANGELES RAMS

Running Back

TODD GURLEY

Date of birth: August 3, 1994 Height: 6 feet, 1 inch (1.85 m) Weight: 224 pounds (102 kg) Drafted in the first round of the 2015 NFL Draft (10th pick overall) by the St. Louis (now Los Angeles) Rams College: University of Georgia

CAREER

GAMES	RUSH	RUYDS	RUTD	REC	REYDS	RETD
58	1042	4547	46	187	1883	10

- Appeared in two Pro Bowls (2015, 2017)
- Named AP NFL Offensive Player of the Year in 2017
- Named AP NFL Offensive Rookie of the Year in 2015
- Named first-team All-Pro in 2017 and 2018
- Named first-team All-SEC in 2012 and second-team All-SEC in 2013
- Played high-school football at Tarboro High School (Tarboro, NC) (Nickname: Vikings), 2008–2011

RUNNING BACK

Gurley led the NFL in touchdowns scored for the 2018-2019 season.

- Was named to the 2015 NFL All-Rookie Team
- Was the NFC (National Football Conference) Offensive Player of the Week:
  - Week 4 (2017)
  - Week 15 (2017)
  - Week 16 (2017)
  - Week 6 (2018)
  - Week 13 (2018)
- Was the NFC Offensive Player of the Month:
  - September 2017
  - December 2017
  - October 2018

Gurley has the ability to score and gain yards, oftentimes leaping over his opponents to accomplish this. He has become an important key to the team's *formula* for success offensively and one of the reasons why the Rams are considered one of the rising franchises in the league, with a chance to be great for a long time. He helped lead the Rams to an appearance in Super Bowl LIII following the 2018 season, where they lost 13-3 to New England. Gurley is an effective runner who helps balance the Rams offense. He has gained a lot of attention for someone who has played only four seasons.

Gurley has put together an impressive list of accomplishments in a relatively short time in the NFL.

As he was coming off a successful rookie season in 2015, Gurley met with some *adversity* in his second year. His performance was significantly worse. Despite this "sophomore slump," he rebounded to turn in his best career season in 2017, rushing for a career best 1,305 yards (1,193.3 m), a league-leading thirteen touchdowns, and winning the AP Offensive Player of the Year award. Gurley continued his pursuit for excellence in 2018, helping charge the Rams to the top of the NFL at 13–3, good for the NFC West division title.

Gurley's body of work, since being drafted in 2015, also includes the following accomplishments:

- Led all rookie running backs in rushing yards with 1,106 (1,011.3 m) in 2015
- Led all rookie running backs in rushing touchdowns with ten in 2015
- Led the league in total touchdowns (rushing and receiving) with nineteen in 2017
- Led the league in all-purpose yards with 2,093 (1,913.8 m) in 2017
- Led the league in rushing TDs and total TDs in the 2018 season

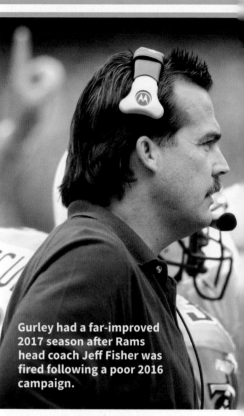

Gurley had a far-improved 2017 season after Rams head coach Jeff Fisher was fired following a poor 2016 campaign.

GURLEY ON THE GRIDIRON

Gurley found the same success that made him an all-state player in high school and two-time all-conference player both in college and in the NFL. He began his career as a member of the St. Louis Rams. The team decided to return to its old home of Los Angeles

Gurley has a long way to go to catch former Ram and Hall of Fame RB Marshall Faulk in the 750/750 category. Faulk hit those marks in four consecutive seasons.

and become the LA Rams for the 2016–2017 NFL season. The change of scenery—as well as some minor conflicts between the team and its head coach Jeff Fisher—may have had an impact on Gurley's performance.

A coaching change for the 2017 season brought a young (the league's youngest head coach) Sean McVay from Washington to Los Angeles. This was followed by a change in quarterbacks, as veteran signal caller Case Keenum went to play for the Minnesota Vikings. This elevated Jared Goff into the starting role and began a partnership that has elevated the passing game, allowing more room for Gurley to operate and help return the Rams to a place as one of the NFL's top teams.

GURLEY'S CAREER STATS

Year	G	Rush Att	Rush Yds	Rush TD	Lng	Y/A	Y/G	Rec	Yds	Y/R	Rec TD	Lng	Fmb
2015	13	229	1106	10	71	4.8	85.1	21	188	9.0	0	31	3
2016	16	278	885	6	24	3.2	55.3	43	327	7.6	0	33	2
2017	15	279	1305	13	57	4.7	87.0	64	788	12.3	6	80	5
2018	14	256	1251	17	36	4.9	89.4	59	580	9.8	4	56	1
Career	56	1042	4,547	46	71	4.4	78.4	187	1,883	10.1	10	80	11

750 / 750 CLUB

Plenty can be said about Gurley's accomplishments in the 2017 season, which won him recognition as the league's best offensive player. He rushed for 1,305 yards (1,193.3 m), thirteen touchdowns, caught the ball sixty-four times for 788 yards (720.5 m), and had 2,093 all-purpose yards (1,913.8 m). He also scored 114 points, which made him the league's highest scorer who was not a placekicker.

LEAPING FOR YARDS

Dancers train for years to execute precisely timed moves. Watching Todd Gurley jump over would-be tacklers while playing the running back position has to make you wonder if he has ever trained as dancer. It's no surprise that he possesses this skill. While in high school, he competed in the 2011 World Youth Championships in both the 110-meters hurdles and 100-meter dash. He posted a personal best of 13.66 seconds in the hurdles, which was good for a third-place finish in the competition's preliminary races. Having world-class speed and hurdling ability means that he probably does not intend to stop jumping over defenders anytime soon.

The effortless way in which Gurley goes over the top of defenders is nothing short of spectacular.

His rushing and receiving totals are eighth all-time on the 750/750 list. Thirteen players are members of the 750/750 club, and former St. Louis Rams running back and Hall of Fame member Marshall Faulk accomplished this feat over four consecutive seasons (1999–2001). Faulk and former San Francisco 49er Roger Craig are the only members of the 1,000/1,000 club.

Player	Team	Year	Rushing	Receiving
Steven Jackson	Saint Louis Rams	2006	1,528	806
Marshall Faulk*	Saint Louis Rams	2001	1,382	765
Marshall Faulk*	Saint Louis Rams	1999	1,381	1,048
Le'Veon Bell	Pittsburgh Steelers	2014	1,361	854
Marshall Faulk*	Saint Louis Rams	2000	1,359	830
Brian Westbrook	Philadelphia Eagles	2007	1,333	771
Marshall Faulk*	Saint Louis Rams	1998	1,319	908
Todd Gurley	Los Angeles Rams	2017	1,305	788
David Johnson	Arizona Cardinals	2016	1,239	879
Marcus Allen*	Los Angeles Raiders	1984	1,168	758
Roger Craig	San Francisco 49ers	1985	1,050	1,016
Matt Forte	Chicago Bears	2014	1,038	808
Charlie Garner	Oakland Raiders	2002	962	941
Joe Washington	Baltimore Colts	1979	884	750
Chet Mutryn	Buffalo Bills	1948	823	794
Charley Taylor	Washington	1964	755	814

*Member of Pro Football Hall of Fame

CLUB RECORD FOR CONSECUTIVE GAMES WITH A TOUCHDOWN

Hall of Fame RB Eric Dickerson is one of the many superstar players in Rams' history.

The Los Angeles Rams have a long and proud history in the NFL. First formed in 1946, the team was part of the western expansion for the league, making the league a true coast-to-coast entity. There are many great names in Rams' history, for Los Angeles, as well as for St. Louis, where the team played in the 1995–2015 NFL seasons. These players include David "Deacon" Jones, Roosevelt "Rosey" Grier, Merlin Olsen, Jack Youngblood, Jim Everett, fellow running backs Eric Dickerson, Steven Jackson, and Elroy "Crazy Legs" Hirsch. Jones, Grier, and Olsen were three-fourths of the famous Rams' Fearsome Foursome defense of the 1960s and 1970s (with Youngblood, a future Hall of Fame member, joining the defensive line in the 1970s).

Hirsch, who was one of the Rams' earliest superstars, played during the 1950s (1949–1957). He received his nickname due to his unconventional running style. Crazy or not, it helped Hirsch find the end zone on a regular and consistent basis and helped him become a member of the Hall of Fame in 1968.

One Rams record that few thought would be surpassed was Hirsch's mark for consecutive games scoring a touchdown. He established the team record during the 1951 season. He scored a touchdown in twelve consecutive games that season. That record stood for sixty-six years until Gurley broke it during the 2017 season. In a division rival matchup against the Seattle Seahawks, which the Rams won 36–31, Gurley rushed for 120 yards (109.7 m) and one touchdown, and the record.

1950's star Elroy "Crazy Legs" Hirsch held the Ram's record for consecutive games with a touchdown before Gurley broke it in 2017.

TEXT-DEPENDENT QUESTIONS:

1. How many times has Gurley been named to the All-Pro team?
2. What year did he win league Offensive Player of the Year honors?
3. What former Rams player did Gurley pass for the team's record for consecutive games with a rushing touchdown?

WORDS TO UNDERSTAND

ARSENAL – a collection or supply of anything

QUIRK – a peculiarity of action, behavior, or personality; mannerism

TRADEMARK – a distinctive mark or feature particularly characteristic of, or identified with, a person or thing

CHAPTER 4

WORDS COUNT

When the time comes to address the media before or after a game, players either retreat to the comfort of traditional phrases that avoid controversy (Cliché City), or they speak their mind with refreshing candor (Quote Machine).

Here are ten Todd Gurley quotes, compiled in part from various websites, including Twitter, with some insight as to the context of what he is talking about or referencing:

At the 2015 NFL Draft, Gurley was not concerned by where he was drafted. He was already looking ahead to succeeding on the field.

I'm not here to be No. 5 overall or a second-round pick. I want to be the best.

Gurley was actually the tenth overall selection of the St. Louis Rams in the 2015 NFL Draft, but being drafted high was not something that he was too concerned with, even though he was the first running back drafted. Gurley set his sights on becoming the best running back in the league regardless of draft position, and worked toward that goal. This quote suggests that he realized the draft was just the beginning, and focused instead on what he wanted to become down the road. If all he wanted was to be a top draft pick, he probably would not have been recognized as the top rookie or the best offensive player in the NFL two years later. **Rating: Quote Machine**

Gurley believes strongly in providing opportunities for youth to learn and have access to books and other learning materials. He supports causes such as First Book, a charity located in Washington, D.C. (see Chapter 5 for more information). He also made the charity his cause as part of the NFL's "My Cause, My Cleats" campaign in 2018. He knows that getting an education requires students to be able to read and communicate effectively through writing. Although this quote is not very illuminating about his motivations, Gurley is committed to using his celebrity as an NFL player to help students learn to read and write. **Rating: Cliché City**

Reading and writing are the keys to education.

> **It's really like a last-minute decision, man. It's what position my body is in, and it's like my last move... I really don't think about it. It really just happens.**

Gurley, in an August 15, 2018, *GQ* magazine interview, discussed his ability to get airborne and leap over his defenders. This ability has become a **trademark** of sorts for him and has created some of his best runs and rushing TDs. Jumping is not something he plans to do but rather something that he just does. It gives him an ability to elude a tackle and turn an ordinary play into something extraordinary for his team. **Rating: Quote Machine**

> **You play for team goals, but who wouldn't want to be the NFL sack leader? Who wouldn't want to be the NFL passing or rushing leader? It's hard to get it.**

Gurley plays for the benefit of his team's success, not necessarily his personal success. That being said, he has been honored with several awards and gained individual recognition in his NFL career. Gurley puts team before self and personal goals when on the field, giving everything he has so the Rams can win. In this quote, he candidly acknowledges that winning honors such as rookie and player of the year are hard to accomplish, and are achievements to be proud of. Gurley has many more honors to come if he continues to play at a high level. **Rating: Quote Machine**

ROOKIE OF THE YEAR ACCEPTANCE SPEECH

Gurley admitted that he was giving his first public speech ever when he was named the AP Offensive Rookie of the Year. Going in front of a crowd of colleagues and fans to accept an award is a tough thing to do. It can be even tougher if you are doing for the first time. Adding to the pressure of giving this type of speech, the Rams had just announced a plan to move from St Louis to Los Angeles, a decision that upset a lot of fans. Gurley addressed this disappointment expressed by the St. Louis fan base and showed that he could do more than rush a football.

Gurley delivered a short and humble speech in accepting his award as the NFL's 2015 Rookie of the Year.

I love cats, though. Cats are so cool. Actually, I'm probably going to get some this year.

Gurley has no problem admitting that he is a "crazy cat dude".

One of Gurley's **quirkier** interests outside of the game of football is his love of cats. He so loves cats that he wants to adopt at least two of them. Gurley has referred to himself as being a "crazy cat dude," a title that he completely accepts and owns. It is unusual for an NFL player (or for many professional athletes in general) to prefer cats to dogs, which he does not like. He stressed his preference with this quote in interview with ESPN. **Rating: Quote Machine**

One day, it's probably going to end bad. Until then, I'm going to keep jumping.

This quote is a reference to his leaps, which he has made a part of his running style. Gurley was a hurdler in high school with world-class skills. This skill has served him well in both college as well as the NFL, as he has used his ability to jump over potential tacklers. It is an ability that he says he uses without much thought because it feels natural to him to simply jump over a player coming at him to make a tackle. Gurley feels that since he is early in his career, he should deploy every weapon in his **arsenal** to help the Rams win. He admits that the longer he jumps over opponents, the greater the potential for him to get injured or for it to end badly. Until that happens, he plans to keep on jumping. **Rating: Quote Machine**

Although he admits that it is a risky maneuver, Gurley says it is instinct from his days on the track to hurdle would-be tacklers.

> **If you can't take care of the ball, then nine times out of ten you're probably going to end up losing—whoever wins the turnover battle, is going to win the game.**

Gurley rarely fumbles the football. At a career rate of 0.01 fumbles per carry, he is one of the most reliable running backs in the league. Taking care of the ball is something that is important to him. Gurley understands that having a low turnover rate gives his team more opportunities to score, or at least to stay in the game and have chances to make big plays to win. Maintaining control of the ball and winning the turnover battle are viewed as important keys to winning games, and this quote repeats a classic coach's cliché that players hear at every level. Gurley has done his part by ensuring the number of turnovers that he commits is one of the lowest in the NFL. **Rating: Cliché City**

He is willing to give credit to all his teammates that contribute to the success of the team. This quote defines his approach to the game and how he sees his role as part of a team as opposed to one of its stars. He has become a successful running back in the NFL, but he is equally happy with celebrating the success of his teammates. Gurley knows that he can be successful only if his QB Jared Goff, for example, is successful. He also knows that he can continue to be successful only if the defensive stars (like DE—defensive end—Aaron Donald) make plays and give the offense the best opportunity to score. It is easy to see that he is genuinely happy for the success of others. **Rating: Quote Machine**

> **I've always been a person to be happy for other people's success.**

Gurley says that his success is only possible when teammates like QB Jared Goff are also successful.

> **It's always good to go back home. Home is where the love is.**

Gurley's was born in Baltimore, MD, and raised in the small community of Tarboro, NC. It is to Tarboro that he has a strong connection, and where he sharpened the skills that have made him the successful player he has become in the NFL. Gurley takes the opportunity to go home whenever he can to be with the family and friends he grew up with. He loves being home because it is the place he can go and not have to be Todd Gurley, star running back for the Los Angeles Rams. He can go back to Tarboro and just be Todd Gurley, son, brother, friend.
Rating: Quote Machine

Gurley has rushed for an average of 4.4 yards (4.0 m) per carry and 79.8 yards (73.0 m) a game. He is used to gaining a lot of yards in a game and averaging a lot of yards per carry. His ability to gain a lot of yards comes from one of the strengths that was identified by scouts during the 2015 NFL Scouting Combine—Gurley's ability to power through initial contact and keep his legs moving to pick up more yards. However, he credits the ability of his teammates to make the blocks that allow him to find openings. Without his upfront blockers or downfield (second-level) blockers like the receivers, he knows he would not be able to achieve the results that he does. **Rating: Quote Machine**

> **"I mean, it's just a whole team effort, and that's what gets those runs—those 10-, 15-, 20-yard runs are from those receivers and those guys blocking on the second level.**

RESEARCH PROJECT:

Staying on the subject of cats, although it is true that most NFL players own dogs, there are others who prefer cats as well. There are several NFL players, in fact, who prefer the company of cats over dogs and are not afraid to show their affection for felines (cats). Perform some research to find out at least five other players who own cats, including the name of their pet.

TEXT-DEPENDENT QUESTIONS:

1. What draft number did the St. Louis Rams use to select Todd Gurley?
2. What type of pet does he prefer to own?
3. What is his career fumble-per-carry rate?

WORDS TO UNDERSTAND

AMENITY – any feature that provides comfort, convenience, or pleasure

CLEATS – a shoe fitted with conical or rectangular projections, usually made of hard rubber, or a metal strip with sharp projections, built into or attached to the sole of a shoe to provide greater traction

GATED COMMUNITY – a residential development that is exclusive to its residents, typically protected by a security fence and a guarded entrance

MOGUL – an important, powerful, or influential person

CHAPTER 5

OFF THE FIELD

GURLEY AT HOME

Gurley took the earnings from his first NFL contract and used them to purchase his first home. This is quite an accomplishment for anybody, but especially for a twenty-two-year-old NFL rookie who grew up in the small town of Tarboro, NC, with a population of over 11,000 residents. He chose to establish roots in the city where he plays football, Los Angeles, in the gated community of Chatsworth.

Gurley lives in one of these gated communities in the Chatsworth neighborhood of Los Angeles.

Gurley purchased a 5,200 square foot Mediterranean-style house for $1.825 million in 2017. The house provides many amenities, but the one of particular importance to a player of his level is the large soaker bathtub that he can use to ease some of the aches, pains, and stress that come with being a star running back.

The home also has five bedrooms and five bathrooms, which are perfect for a future family of his own or when his parents and siblings come to visit. A swimming pool with a built-in water slide and barbeque pit complete the amenities and are fitting for this star on the rise.

THE IMPORTANCE OF EDUCATION

Gurley left school at the University of Georgia (located in Athens, GA) in his junior year and entered the 2015 NFL Draft. His decision to leave school was fueled in part by his four-game suspension by the NCAA for accepting payments connected to the sale of his autographs and signed memorabilia. The loss of Gurley from the Bulldogs roster (he was a potential Heisman Award winner in 2014 before deciding to turn professional) even caused the Georgia legislature to pass a law making it a crime to encourage student-athletes to break NCAA rules, punishable by a year in prison.

Although Gurley has not graduated from college (and has not announced whether he plans to return to Georgia, or another school, after his playing days are over), he is passionate about making educational opportunities available to all school-aged children. Gurley is particularly concerned about leveling the playing field for kids in disadvantaged areas by providing them with books and learning aids that encourage reading.

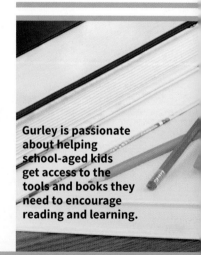

Gurley is passionate about helping school-aged kids get access to the tools and books they need to encourage reading and learning.

#WHATSYOURSTORY - FIRST BOOK CHILDHOOD LITERACY PROJECT AND PIZZA HUT

For the 2018 season, the NFL unveiled its "My Cause, My Cleats," campaign. During the second week of December (December 13–December 17), players wore specifically designed cleats that displayed a cause that they are passionate about. For Gurley, that cause is childhood literacy and access to books. He wore cleats that display his support for the First Book organization. First Book is a Washington, DC–based nonprofit that, since 1992, has distributed more than 175 million books to children in need across the country. The aim of the organization is to provide books and other educational materials to those who may not otherwise have access to these learning resources. Having Gurley and his cleats representing First Book should bring a lot of attention to the issue of childhood literacy and educational opportunities for all.

Todd Gurley visited local elementary school in partnership with Pizza Hut BOOK IT! to create equal access to quality education

Players were given the opportunity to display their causes, and Gurley, along with the help of Pizza Hut, drove donations of $1 for each book bundle given to the First Book organization.

Shriners Hospital for Children is an organization Gurley cares deeply about supporting.

IN THE COMMUNITY

INSPIRING FANS TO GIVE

One of Gurley's fans, Jeff Fell, was so encouraged by Gurley's philanthropy and willingness to give that he stepped up to show his support for one of Gurley's causes, Shriners Hospital for Children. Shriners is an organization that operates twenty-two hospitals across the United States, including one location in Montreal, Quebec, Canada. The purpose of the Shriners is to provide hospital care for children in need, regardless of their ability to pay. No child in need of medical attention is turned away.

Shriners is a charity that is near and dear to Gurley's heart. As a high-school senior in 2011, he had the opportunity to star in the Shrine Bowl of the Carolinas All-Star game and showcase his talents as a running back (and future star). This connection with the Shriners has turned into a lifelong commitment to give and provide support for the Shriners cause.

Fell, who participated in fantasy football as a team owner, won the top prize in his league. This was accomplished with the help of Gurley's performance in the 2017–2018 season, which led to his winning the league's Offensive Player of the Year award. Fell decided to pay it forward by donating his winnings to the Shriners Hospital for Children.

Fell included Gurley in a tweet dated December 26, 2017, by noting, "*Only fair to give something back, right @TG3II?*" Gurley was touched by the move and reached out to Fell with the message, "*Fantasy is not so bad after all lol that's major Love. Thank you and Happy Holidays.*" Several other fantasy team players, inspired by Gurley's 2017 season also made donations to the Shriners Hospital for Children. A total of $10,500 in donations were sent, showing the influence he has over his fans to join him in supporting the community.

GIVING BACK

Gurley served as an honorary chairman of the annual Taste of the Rams charity event in November 2018. The fundraiser brought together 400 individuals from the greater Los Angeles community and raised nearly $500,000 overall, $170,000 of which went to provide nearly 2 million meals for the Los Angeles Regional Food Bank. He also spends much of his time and effort donating money to schools, and he also gave new athletic equipment to his old school, Tarboro High School.

Volunteers sort donations at the Los Angeles Regional Food Bank. Gurley helped to raise $170,000 for the organization in 2018.

THE MARKETING OF TODD GURLEY

Gurley's agent is Ari Nissim of Roc Nation Sports. Roc Nation is a sports and talent agency that was formed in 2013 as a partnership between Creative Artists Agency and rap **mogul** Shawn "Jay-Z" Carter. Being a part of Roc Nation has given Gurley exposure to many national and international brands. He, along with teammates QB Jared Goff and DE Aaron Donald are the face of Los Angeles Rams. Playing for a team that is in the number two media buying market in the U.S. means sponsors want to have a player of Gurley's caliber on their side.

Some of the brands that have signed deals with Gurley include Pizza Hut, Gatorade, and Nike. He has also been signed on as a spokesperson for Carl's Jr., Bose speakers, and

Campbell's Chunky Soup. As he gains more yards and perhaps wins championships for Los Angeles, Gurley's marketing brand will grow to approach those of the other great athletes competing in the city, like NBA (National Basketball Association) star LeBron James of the LA Lakers.

SALARY INFORMATION

Gurley was drafted by the then St. Louis Rams with the tenth pick of the 2015 NFL Draft. He signed a rookie contract for four years (2015–2018) for a total value of $13.8 million. Gurley later reworked the last year of the contract, which resulted in a nearly $3 million raise.

YEAR	SALARY	ROSTER BONUS	SIGNING BONUS	TOTAL
2015	$435,000	$0	$2,078,306	$2,513,306
2016	$1,063,326	$0	$2,078,306	$3,141,632
2017	$1,691,653	$0	$2,078,306	$3,769,959
2018*	$2,319,979	$0	~~$2,078,306~~	$4,398,285
TOTAL	$5,509,958	$0	$8,313,224	$13,823,182

*New contract in 2018:

YEAR	SALARY	ROSTER BONUS	SIGNING BONUS	TOTAL
2018	$950,000	$0	$6,278,306	$7,228,306
TOTAL	$950,000	$0	$6,278,306	$7,228,306

Gurley signed a five-year salary extension on July 24, 2018, worth $59 million in salary and roster bonuses, plus an additional $16.8 million in signing bonuses. The contract keeps him in a Rams uniform until at least 2022, with an additional year (2023) worth $10.5 million if he chooses to stay in Los Angeles.

YEAR	SALARY	ROSTER BONUS	SIGNING BONUS	TOTAL
2019	$5,000,000	$0	$4,200,000	$9,200,000
2020	$5,500,000	$7,550,000	$4,200,000	$17,250,000
2021	$4,000,000	$5,000,000	$4,200,000	$13,200,000
2022	$5,000,000	$5,000,000	$4,200,000	$14,200,000
2023	$5,449,979	$5,000,000	$0	$10,449,979
TOTAL	$24,949,979	$22,550,000	$16,800,000	$64,299,979

There is no doubt that Gurley has all the tools necessary for a long and successful NFL career. He has been rewarded with a large contract that will keep him in one of the country's top markets for years. Gurley may eventually stop leaping defenders so much to preserve himself a bit and add a few more years to his NFL career. Whatever he decides to do, Gurley has clearly put himself on a path to greatness that will have his name spoken alongside those of the greatest running backs in NFL history.

Sports equipment and apparel giant Nike is just one of several brands Gurley endorses.

RESEARCH PROJECT:

Giving back to the community is something successful professional athletes strive to do. Whether it is through a personal foundation to which money can be given to different causes of interest, or by forming a charity that can impact lives locally, regionally, nationally, or even globally, athletes are in a unique position to impact lives and make changes. Gurley has embraced this notion and has used his fame and wealth to help the community, especially where children are involved.

Find three other NFL players who recently spent time connecting with the residents of their city after a disaster, such as a fire or hurricane, and not only wrote a check but also rolled up their sleeves and helped. List the event, describe the efforts that were made in each case, and detail how much money was raised.

TEXT-DEPENDENT QUESTIONS:

1. Gurley signed a contract in 2018 for four years, more than $59 million, and additional $16.8 million in signing bonuses. How much signing bonus will he receive in each year of the four-year deal?

2. In which community did Gurley purchase his first home? How much did he pay for the house?

3. What is the name of the cause that he supported during the NFL's 2018 "My Cause, My Cleats" campaign?

blitz – a defensive strategy in which one or more linebackers or defensive backs, in addition to the defensive line, attempt to overwhelm the quarterback's protection by attacking from unexpected locations or situations.

cornerbacks – the defenders primarily responsible for preventing the offenses wide receivers from catching passes, accomplished by remaining as close to the opponent as possible during pass routes. Cornerbacks are usually the fastest players on the defense.

defensive backs – a label applied to cornerbacks and safeties, or the secondary in general.

end zone – an area 10 yards deep at either end of the field bordered by the goal line and the boundaries.

field goal – an attempt to kick the ball through the uprights, worth three points. It is taken by a specialist called the *place kicker*. Distances are measured from the spot of the kick plus 10 yards for the depth of the end zone.

first down – the first play in a set of four downs, or when the offense succeeds in covering 10 yards in the four downs.

fumble – when a player loses possession of the ball before being tackled, normally by contact with an opponent. Either team may recover the ball. The ground cannot cause a fumble.

goal line – the line that divides the end zones from the rest of the field. A touchdown is awarded if the ball breaks the vertical plane of the goal line while in possession or if a receiver catches the ball in the end zone.

huddle – a gathering of the offense or defense to communicate the upcoming play decided by the coach.

interception – a pass caught by a defensive player instead of an offensive receiver. The ball may be returned in the other direction.

lateral – a pass or toss behind the originating player to a teammate as measured by the lines across the field. Although the offense may only make one forward pass per play, there is no limit to the number of laterals at any time.

line of scrimmage – an imaginary line, determined by the ball's location before each play, that extends across the field from sideline to sideline. Seven offensive players must be on the line of scrimmage, though the defense can set up in any formation. Forward passes cannot be thrown from beyond the line of scrimmage.

pass – when the ball is thrown to a receiver who is farther down the field. A team is limited to one such forward pass per play. Normally this is the duty of the quarterback, although technically any eligible receiver can pass the ball.

play action – a type of offensive play in which the quarterback pretends to hand the ball to a running back before passing the ball. The goal is to fool the secondary into weakening their pass coverage.

play clock – visible behind the end zone at either end of the stadium. Once a play is concluded, the offense has 40 seconds to snap the ball for the next play. The duration is reduced to 25 seconds for game-related stoppages such as penalties. Time is kept on the play clock. If the offense does not snap the ball before the play clock elapses, they incur a five-yard penalty for delay of game.

punt – a kick, taken by a special teams player called the *punter*, that surrenders possession to the opposing team. This is normally done on fourth down when the offense deems gaining a first down unlikely.

receiver – an offensive player who may legally catch a pass, almost always a wide receiver, tight end, or running back. Only the two outermost players on either end of the line of scrimmage—even wide receivers who line up distantly from the offensive line—or the four players behind the line of scrimmage (such as running backs, another wide receiver, and the quarterback) are eligible receivers. If an offensive lineman, normally an ineligible receiver, is placed on the outside of the line of scrimmage because of an unusual formation, he is considered eligible but must indicate his eligibility to game officials before the play.

run – a type of offensive play in which the quarterback, after accepting the ball from center, either keeps it and heads upfield or gives the ball to another player, who then attempts to move ahead with the help of blocking teammates.

sack – a play in which the defense tackles the quarterback behind the line of scrimmage on a pass play.

safety – 1) the most uncommon scoring play in football. When an offensive player is tackled in his own end zone, the defensive team is awarded two points and receives the ball via a kick; 2) a defensive secondary position divided into two roles, free safety and strong safety.

snap – the action that begins each play. The center must snap the ball between his legs, usually to the quarterback, who accepts the ball while immediately behind the center or several yards farther back in a formation called the *shotgun*.

special teams – the personnel that take the field for the punts, kickoffs, and field goals, or a generic term for that part of the game.

tackle – 1) a term for both an offensive and defensive player. The offensive tackles line up on the outside of the line, but inside the tight end, while the defensive tackles protect the interior of their line; 2) the act of forcing a ball carrier to touch the ground with any body part other than the hand or feet. This concludes a play.

tight end – an offensive player who normally lines up on the outside of either offensive tackle. Multiple tight ends are frequently employed on running plays where the offense requires only a modest gain. Roles vary between blocking or running pass routes.

touchdown – scored when the ball breaks the vertical plane of the goal line. Worth six points, and the scoring team can add a single additional point by kick or two points by converting from the two-yard line with an offensive play.

RESOURCES

FURTHER READING

Downs, Michael and Jim Hock, *Hollywood's Team*. Los Angeles: Rare Bird Books, 2016.

Horton, Tim, *Complete Running Back*. Champaign, IL: Human Kinetics, 2018.

Morey, Allan, *The Los Angeles Rams Story*. Minnetonka, MN: Bellweather Media, 2016.

Paris, Jay, *Game of My Life Rams: Memorable Stories of Rams Football.* New York: Skyhorse Publishing Company, Incorporated, 2017.

Turner, Robert W., II, *Not for Long: The Life and Career of the NFL Athlete*. New York: Oxford University Press, 2018.

INTERNET RESOURCES

https://www.pro-football-reference.com/players/G/GurlTo01.htm

The football-specific resource provided by Sports Reference LLC for current and historical statistics of Todd Gurley.

https://www.latimes.com/sports/rams/

The webpage of the *Los Angeles Times* newspaper for the Los Angeles Rams football team.

www.espn.com/nfl/team/_/name/lar/los-angeles-rams

The official website of ESPN sports network for the Los Angeles Rams.

www.nfl.com/

The official website of the National Football League.

https://www.therams.com/

The official NFL website for the Los Angeles Rams football team, including history, player information, statistics, and news.

INDEX

PHOTO CREDITS

Chapter 1

Mario957 / Wikipedia Commons
Royalbroil / Wikipedia Commons
Mario957 / Wikipedia Commons
20614894 © Benkrut - Dreamstime.com

Chapter 2

PA Images / Alamy Stock Photo
Thompson20192 / Flickr
Mario957 / Wikipedia Commons
Thompson200 / Wikipedia Commons
ID 125941216 © David Wood | Dreamstime.com
Thompson200 / Wikipedia Commons
Keith Allison / Flickr
Steve Schar / Flickr
100696270 © Luckyphotographer | Dreamstime.com

Chapter 3

Cal Sport Media / Alamy Stock Photo
Cal Sport Media / Alamy Stock Photo
PA Images / Alamy Stock Photo
Cal Sport Media / Alamy Stock Photo
ID 74218072 © Jerry Coli | Dreamstime.com
ID 37253375 © Jerry Coli | Dreamstime.com
ID 73756453 © Jerry Coli | Dreamstime.com
Elroy Hirsch / Wikipedia Commons

Chapter 4

PA Images / Alamy Stock Photo
12364205 © R. Gino Santa Maria / Shutterfree, Llc | Dreamstime.com
swimfinfan / Wikimedia Commons
10830682 © Connect1 | Dreamstime.com
ID 38840505 © Isselee | Dreamstime.com
Cal Sport Media / Alamy Stock Photo
Jeffrey Beall / Wikipedia Commons

Chapter 5

Cal Sport Media / Alamy Stock Photo
ID 132663432 © trekandshoot | Dreamstime.com
ID 9943765 © Rosemary Buffoni | Dreamstime.com
ID 49420112 © Feng Cheng | Dreamstime.com
petty Officer 1st Class SondraKay Kneen/ Wikipedia Commons
ID 19447540 © Zllgzxy894 | Dreamstime.com

EDUCATIONAL VIDEO LINKS

ABOUT THE AUTHOR

Donald Parker is a father, an author, and an avid sports fan. He enjoys every type of professional sport, including NFL, NBA, MLB, and European club soccer. He enjoyed a brief career as a punter and a defensive back at the NCAA Division III level and now spends much of his time watching and writing about the sports he loves.